Original title:
The Ocean's Silent Whisper

Copyright © 2025 Creative Arts Management OÜ
All rights reserved.

Author: Levi Montgomery
ISBN HARDBACK: 978-1-80587-406-5
ISBN PAPERBACK: 978-1-80587-876-6

The Gentle Sway

The water winks in gleeful play,
As fish do dance in the light of day.
The seaweed sways with fashion flair,
While crabs strut by without a care.

A dolphin jumps with a joyful squeak,
It flips and flops, oh what a freak!
The waves can't stop their bubbling laugh,
As shells gather for a beachy staff.

Reflections in the Tidepool

In pools of glass, the stars do sink,
A crab with sass gives me a wink.
The sea anemone starts to tickle,
As tiny fish play hide and sickle.

The starfish wears a polka dot,
While snails slide by, quite nonchalant.
In this waterworld, life is grand,
A comedy show, all unplanned.

Distant Horizons of Stillness

The sun sets low, with colors bright,
A seagull's hiccup gives me a fright.
As waves crash down, they whisper jokes,
About silly fish and washing folks.

On distant shores, the laughter flows,
Where mermaids sing, and nobody knows.
They juggle shells and tie their hair,
A funny business, with style to spare.

A Symphony of Seabirds

With flapping wings, they hit the high notes,
As gulls rehearse their ocean quotes.
The pelicans dive with a belly flop,
While puffins chat and never stop.

A chorus forms as tides respond,
In funny flaps, they make their pond.
With feathers ruffled, they take a bow,
A comical crew, no doubt, no how!

Tides of Tranquility

A crab named Fred wore a bright-red hat,
He danced with the fish as they all said, "Scat!"
The seagulls laughed, but he didn't care,
He waved his claws, said, "Do I look rare?"

A jellyfish joined, twirling with glee,
"Look at my moves! I'm the star of the sea!"
But then it got stuck in some kelp on the floor,
And everyone else just laughed even more.

Secrets Beneath the Blue

A dolphin named Dave told a whale a tale,
About a lost treasure and a tiny snail.
"I found it once, but I slipped on a rock,"
"And now it just sits in a clam's slimy sock!"

The whale laughed out loud, causing quite a scene,
"That sock's full of pearls, it's a sight to be seen!"
They planned a grand party with snacks made of sea,
While crab cakes danced on the plate—just for free.

Echoes of the Deep

An octopus twirled in a pink polka dot dress,
Each tentacle waving, she looked quite a mess.
"I'm off to a ball under waves so sublime,"
But slipped on some seaweed—oh, what a crime!

The fish all giggled as she swirled around,
"Careful, dear friend! The ocean's renowned!"
A turtle said slowly, munching on kelp,
"Dance like there's no one, just be yourself!"

Murmurs from the Abyss

A pufferfish puffed, in a club made of shells,
He played funky tunes, heard ringing like bells.
The sea urchins bounced, joined in for a cheer,
While clams all sang out, "We've nothing to fear!"

The starfish showed off her fantastic new moves,
"Just watch as I twirl! Now, everybody grooves!"
But right when she leaped, she fell on a stone,
And all the sea life just sighed, "You are prone!"

Stillness Beneath Blue Skies

A seagull steals my sandwich, what a cheek!
I thought I was the king of this beach peak.
But here I am, the great crumb chaser,
With bread in hand, I feel like a spacer.

The sun's too bright, I squint and pretend,
That I'm on vacation—oh please, let it end!
But my friend's out surfing, catching a wave,
While I'm here sunbathing, bold and brave.

The shells laugh at me, they roll and spin,
As I trip on a sand dune, let the giggles begin!
A crab walks by, giving me the eye,
I'm pretty sure it's judging my tie-dye.

But as the tide rolls in, I feel so light,
I join the salty dance, it's sheer delight.
With laughter echoing, I join the fun,
In this land of whimsy, I'm never done.

Secrets in the Foam

In bubbly waves, I find a sock,
A treasure from the shore—what a shock!
Did it just escape from someone's foot?
Or join the fish, feeling cute and astute?

A bottle rolls by, it's quite a sight,
It whispers "Help!" in the moonlight.
I'm here with my snacks and a beach ball too,
This is no SOS, just a protein chew!

The tide brings gossip, oh what a tease,
The fish chat about us, with such ease.
With sandy toes, I throw in a shell,
And let the waves carry my wish, oh well!

Laughter mingles with the splashes and shouts,
As we share crazy tales, no doubts sprout.
Secrets in the foam, what a wild ride,
Who knew the ocean had so much pride?

Driftwood Dreams

I found a piece of driftwood, quite bizarre,
It's shaped like a dog, or a rusty car!
With a wink to a crab, I give it a name,
Sir Barkington the wooden—what a claim to fame!

We build a castle, just me and my friend,
Using glue and a dash of luck to blend.
But the waves crash down with a roaring cheer,
And our masterpiece shifts—oh, the end is near!

Sandcastle competition, oh, what a sight!
With buckets and shovels, we go full might.
But Sir Barkington's lost in the swell,
Now he's just a story we'll tell so well.

Yet laughter persists amid our sea fight,
With salt in our hair, and hearts feeling light.
Driftwood dreams never fade with the night,
For joy lives on where the sea is bright.

Glistening Depths

Underneath the waves, I spy a shell,
That glitters and glistens, casting a spell.
But as I reach down, what do I see?
A fish in a suit, sipping iced tea!

He winks at me, and takes a big slurp,
While I stand there confused, feeling like a burp.
"Join my party!" he chirps with glee,
But I'm not sure how to swim, oh wee!

A dolphin flips by, doing a jig,
While sea turtles snap selfies, oh so big.
I laugh in the depths, what a silly sight,
Never knew the fish were so polite!

As bubbles rise fast, I bid adieu,
To this underwater gala, what a crew!
With laughter bubbling like the ocean's song,
Who knew such fun could ever last long?

Lighthouses and Longing

A lighthouse stands, tall and bright,
Hoping to guide boats through the night.
But seagulls laugh at its lonely post,
'Is it love or just toast?'

Waves crash down with a hearty cheer,
Splashes of water, a slippery sphere.
The lighthouse shouts, 'Hey, watch your shoes!'
But the fish below just giggle and snooze.

Beneath a Veil of Water

A crab in a tux, what a sight to behold,
Dancing around, not caring, so bold.
With a wave and a clap, it throws a grand ball,
But the fish are too busy to come at all.

An octopus knocks on a clam's cozy door,
'Come out, dear friend, let's have some more!'
But the clam just grumbles, 'I'm snug and I'm tired,'
While the octo dreams of a party inspired.

Reflections of Serenity

The waves whisper jokes in a soft, breezy tone,
While starfish giggle, wiggling alone.
A dolphin flips high, with a splash and a twirl,
Yelling, 'Catch me, you landlubber girl!'

Seaweed sways with a shimmy and shake,
'I'm just trying to dance; it's not a mistake!'
But the turtles look on, their faces perplexed,
'We prefer naps over that kind of text!'

In the Wake of the Tide

A fish with a hat, swimming with flair,
Says, 'If I don't have style, then who really cares?'
The crabs high-five with their pinchers so spry,
As a whale glides by, singing, 'Oh my!'

Ripples of laughter bounce off the shore,
Seashells conspire, 'Let's open a store!'
They sell sea jokes and riddles galore,
While the tide rolls in, bringing fun and more!

The Calm of Twilight Waters

In twilight's glow, the sea does yawn,
A fish once told me, "Hey, I'm drawn!"
To swim in circles, not a care,
While seagulls squawk and steal my share.

A boat drifts by, with sails so bright,
But don't ask me if they're adjusting right.
The captain's lost, his map's all wet,
He follows waves like a brave marionette.

A whale waves back, with a cheeky grin,
"What's up, landfish? Want to join in?"
But I just laugh, he's way too big,
Instead, I'll stick to my fancy twig.

So as the stars begin to gleam,
I gather shells; it's quite the dream.
With bubbles rising, I begin to sing,
In this calm, odd little seafaring ring.

Gulls Cry Over Silent Seas

On rocky shores, those gulls convene,
Debating fish and who's the queen.
One swoops low with a sassy flare,
"You can't catch me! I'm up in the air!"

They steal my fries, oh what a sight!
I chase them down, oh what a fight!
But they just squawk and flap away,
Those feathered thieves are here to stay.

Beneath the waves, the crabs are sly,
Plotting revenge as I pass by.
They chuckle soft, in their sandy dens,
"Let's trap the human! Make him spend!"

So here I am, defending my lunch,
With pesky gulls and crabs that punch.
The silent seas can only shake,
While I enjoy my oceanic cake.

Where Dreams Drift Away

Out where the waves tickle the shore,
I spotted a starfish, quite a bore.
"Dream big!" he said, with a lazy wave,
But I prefer snacks, and that's how I save.

A dolphin danced with a tiny splash,
Tried to show off, but he fell with a crash.
"Just keep on swimming," the seaweed said,
But all I could think about was bread.

With jellyfish wiggling, in a slow jam,
I did a little dance—what a clam!
They wobbled back, with a jelly-like tease,
"Join our party, we've got the cheese!"

As sun dips low, I start to dream,
Of crispy chips and an ice cream beam.
The waves keep whispering, "Stay, play along,"
But my heart beats louder, "Sing your own song!"

A Sea of Serenity

In waters calm, the fish have fun,
Each tiny scale shines like the sun.
They gossip soft, about their day,
"Did you see that crab? He's so cliché!"

A turtle rolls by, smooth and slow,
He waves a flipper—he's the star of the show.
"Race me!" I shout, he laughs with glee,
"Just give me a moment, I'm drinking sea tea!"

Bubbles rise, like little balloons,
Dancing merrily with the afternoon tunes.
A mermaid giggles as I dive down,
Rejecting my help, she'll wear that crown!

At day's end, I chuckle with joy,
The sea holds secrets, like a friendly toy.
With every ripple and wave that sways,
This endless laughter, in so many ways.

The Land of Forgotten Currents

In a realm where fish wear hats,
And crabs have secret chats,
The waves gossip with a giggle,
While seaweed does a jolly wiggle.

Starfish dance on sandy shores,
Chasing after seagull roars,
An octopus tries to juggle shells,
While clam shells sing their silly bells.

Jellyfish bounce like balloons,
Underneath the laughing moons,
And turtles race in tiny cars,
While dolphins strum their fishy guitars.

In this land that rarely sleeps,
Mermaids trade in silly leaps,
For laughter floats on every tide,
In waves where joy and whimsy ride.

The Cry of the Distant Siren

A siren sings from rocks so high,
With a voice that makes fish fry,
She calls to sailors with a grin,
But forgets her sunscreen, oh what a sin!

Her hair like seaweed, tangles fierce,
While her laughter makes the dolphins pierce,
She winks at boats with a playful shout,
And tells the crew to twist and shout.

Sea gulls join in, they take a stand,
Dancing on waves like a marching band,
And as her song twists like a spree,
All the crabs tap dance in glee.

Yet when she slips on seaweed's throne,
The ocean echoes her funny groan,
And all the waves start to quiver,
At the sight of her slippery sliver.

Mysterious Waters

Bubbles pop like tiny dreams,
As fish plot silly little schemes,
They wear sunglasses, oh so cool,
And glide past seaweed like a pool.

A treasure chest with candy treats,
Where mermaids snack on gummy sweets,
Octopuses playing poker too,
While turtles judge from the ocean blue.

The deep sea whispers cheesy tales,
Of pirates lost in jelly trails,
And every wave gives a hearty chuckle,
As whales join in for a giggly huddle.

In these waters, laughter flows,
With playful currents that tickle toes,
So if you dive and feel the cheer,
Just know the fun is always near.

Drift into the Depths

Drifting down to depths unknown,
Where bubbles float and laughter's sown,
A pufferfish dons a top hat neat,
And shrimp put on a tap dance feat.

The sea urchins throw a bash,
With disco lights, they twist and flash,
A crab DJ spins the tunes,
As sea cucumbers dance 'neath moons.

Fish in tuxedos glide and glide,
While eels pull pranks from every side,
In this realm of mirthful play,
Where sea creatures find their way.

So come aboard and float with glee,
Join the dance beneath the sea,
For in these depths, the joy won't stop,
As laughter echoes, on and on, it'll plop!

Echoes Along the Shoreline

Seagulls squawk and dance in air,
While crabs wear suits with no despair.
The sandcastles fall, yet we persist,
With tiny moats that twist and twist.

Waves crash and giggle, splashing all,
Shells roll in like a carnival ball.
A beach ball bounces, kids start to scream,
Chasing their friends—a slippery dream.

Sunburned noses on a quest for fun,
Ice cream melts as we run and run.
Footprints vanish with each silly wave,
Making memories, bold and brave.

The whispers of seashells tell a tale,
Of fish in tuxedos, without fail.
As laughter echoes along the sand,
Creating joy, so close at hand.

In the Embrace of Waves

In foamy chairs made of seaweed green,
Where dolphins tease with a playful scene.
A sun hat floats—oh, what a sight!
While jellyfish glide, what a funny flight.

A picnic feast, with sandwiches wide,
Seagulls swoop with an ambitious glide.
We share our fries, they steal our hopes,
As we try to catch the slippery slopes.

Beach towels flutter like flags on the run,
As sandcastles crumble, a laugh, just for fun.
Coconuts roll, playing hide and seek,
While sunburns tease with a tint so bleak.

But with each splash, we find pure delight,
In the laughter that warms us, day and night.
So here in the surf, we continue to play,
Embracing the waves, come what may.

The Mystery of Tidal Dreams

Caught in a whirl of sandy mysteries,
Where jellybeans hide among the seas.
Fish in bowties swim past our knees,
Trading chuckles like a summer breeze.

Seashells giggle when they're in a rush,
Waves whisper secrets, creating a hush.
A crab recites poetry, oh so grand,
While sea turtles breakdance on the sand.

The tide steps back, then comes on the chase,
Waves tickle toes; we jump with grace.
A treasure map leads to candy canes,
Underneath where the turtle remains.

In the rhythm of splashes, we find our tune,
As laughter rises to meet the moon.
With sandy toes and salty air,
We dream of mermaids, swimming somewhere.

A Haven Underneath the Blue

Beneath the azure, fish wear bright hats,
While octopuses play jump rope with their spats.
A treasure chest filled with shiny things,
And clams that gossip of undersea flings.

The dolphins with sunglasses, oh so chic,
Pose for selfies—their latest peak.
While coral reefs whisper tales of delight,
Of parties held under the pale moonlight.

A lobster joins in with the dance of the tide,
As squids in tuxedos take a joyride.
Bubble parties rise to the hum of the sea,
As we laugh and delight, so wild and free.

So here is our haven, where fun finds its way,
In the blue depths where we wish to stay.
With every splash, we craft our dreams,
In this vibrant world, where joy always beams.

Tranquil Ripples

A fish once wore a tiny hat,
It swam around, oh what of that!
With bubbles bursting, it would dance,
The ocean laughed, a jiggy prance.

A crab wore shades upon its eyes,
While seahorses chatted with surprise.
They threw a party on the sand,
With seaweed snacks, all quite unplanned.

A starfish tried to grab the mic,
But slipped off rocks—it wasn't like!
It tumbled down, much to our glee,
The sea sang songs of jubilee.

With barnacles singing off-key tunes,
And dolphins spinning, making boons.
The playful tide rolled in and out,
In a giddy sea of laughter, no doubt!

Secrets of the Salted Breeze

A seagull squawked with sass and flair,
It claimed the beach, but found a snare.
Chasing after chips with great delight,
It snatched a fry and took to flight.

A clam, so shy, penned little notes,
To share with friends, in cozy boats.
But when it tried to spread its word,
The waves just giggled, 'How absurd!'

A jellyfish wore a sparkly dress,
It waved hello, in jelly mess.
The ocean teased, "Your dance is grand!"
While all the fish just took a stand.

With mermaids laughing on their phones,
They shared selfies with fishy drones.
The tides rolled in, a party spree,
With secrets shared, so joyously!

Veiled Conversations of the Waves

In rippling hues, the sea did chat,
With shells and stones, none were a brat.
"Hey, did you hear?" a wave would chime,
"Last night I saw a fish with a rhyme!"

They whispered tales of sunken loot,
And sea turtles in goofy suits.
A clownfish joked, "Where's my stand-up?"
But fish just floated, the tide was plump.

A blowfish puffed, "I'm quite the star!"
While barnacles played a sea guitar.
The kelp joined in with leafy notes,
In this watery world, laughter floats.

The currents carried their giddy fun,
Comedic waves under the sun.
In salty whispers, joy would thrive,
Where humor swam, all was alive!

Mysteries in the Mist

Beneath the fog, a strange sight lurked,
A squid in boots, it truly worked!
It guided boats with ink so bold,
While tales of mischief began to unfold.

A dolphin slid in, wearing a tie,
"Who invited the octopus?" it did spy.
"Not me!" exclaimed the lobster with glee,
"Let's dance with the kraken, just wait and see!"

Underneath the misty arena,
A whale did twist, the grand ballerina.
Twirls and swirls, the seashells clapped,
As fish gathered 'round, hilariously rapped.

With every wave, the laughter swelled,
In salty mists, funny stories dwelled.
From currents playful, no tale's too grand,
In the silliness, all of sea's a band!

Harmony in Hushed Depths

Bubbles rise in laughter's tune,
Fish gossip under the pale moon.
Jellyfish dancing, swirl like a pro,
Seaweed wigs in the current flow.

Turtles race with a silly grin,
While crabs on the sand hop in a spin.
A sea cucumber trips and falls,
Even the starfish giggles in the calls.

Seagulls squawk secrets of the tide,
While dolphins breakdance, bursting with pride.
Clams snap shut with a bashful chime,
As whales hum their jokes, one at a time.

Underwater parties, a zany delight,
With octopuses painting the world bright.
A conch shell wears a top hat, it's true,
In the depths of the sea, you'd laugh too!

Nautical Secrets Unveiled

Sailors tell tales of squids with style,
Who waltz through the waves with elegant guile.
A fish in a tuxedo, so dapper and neat,
Wants everyone to join in for a sea-side treat.

Starfish wear sunglasses, looking so grand,
While lobsters serve snacks, a shellfish band.
Puffer fish puff up, like balloons in flight,
Making the jokes take off into the night.

A crab with a cane prances down the shore,
Chasing seagulls, begging for just one more.
Bubbles pop like laughter, you can hear all around,
As anchovies moonwalk on the sandy ground.

With treasure maps marked by 'x' of delight,
Octopi plotting their next comic bite.
When fish play charades, it's quite the show,
Secrets of the sea, who would've known?

Shadows on the Sand

Footprints dance in the twilight glow,
A crab's audition for a cameo.
Seashells gather round for a cheer,
As wave after wave brings laughter near.

A starfish struts with a sassy pose,
While pelicans bring pies, much to their doze.
Kites fly high, with tails of the sea,
While dolphins clap in glee, can you see?

Sandcastles taller than kings on high,
Decorated with shells that dare touch the sky.
The ocean giggles in a playful dance,
As sunbeams wiggle, giving us a chance.

In shadows that stretch as the day draws near,
The whispers of laughter are all that we hear.
Seagulls play tag, chasing dreams on the breeze,
Oh, the joy of the shore, like a life filled with cheese!

The Calm Before the Surge

The water's still with a cheeky grin,
As tide pools whisper, 'Let the fun begin!'
Seasick fish in their bubble suits,
Dare to wiggle in polka-dot boots.

Crabs throw a party with feisty flair,
Waving their claws like they just don't care.
Anemones giggle as they sway to the beat,
Winking at driftwood while keeping it neat.

Surfers stand ready, waiting to glide,
With hopes that the waves will be on their side.
A seal pops up with a splash and a roar,
'Surf's up!' he howls from the ocean floor.

In the hush before chaos, there's laughter galore,
As creatures of the sea gather by the shore.
The calm holds secrets in its funny embrace,
For soon all will frolic in this wild, splashy place!

Waves of Serenity

The waves they crash, but oh so slow,
They tease the shore with a gentle flow.
They tickle toes and dance around,
While seagulls squawk, a silly sound.

Fishes splash, with a flick of their tails,
They chuckle at jellyfish in their veils.
Shells whisper secrets, they can't be shy,
While crabs do the tango, oh my, oh my!

A beach ball bounces with glee and flair,
Sandy castles rise, up to the air.
The sunbeams giggle, warming our feet,
What's that in the distance? A surfboard fleet!

Laughter echoes, with a salty mist,
Every grain of sand has a sun-kissed twist.
We dance with the tides, carefree and light,
In this world of whimsy, everything's right.

Quiet Currents

Whispers come from the deep blue sea,
A fish with glasses texts a selfie.
Starfish pose, oh so bizarre,
While sea cucumbers dream of a car.

Turtles surf on the gentle swell,
Telling tales of a fantastical shell.
Octopuses juggle with eight crafty hands,
And plankton dances, making big plans.

The current giggles, tickling our toes,
A whale shows off in a pirouette pose.
Seashells gossip about the lot,
As dolphins leap, giving it all they've got.

Aquatic humor fills the air,
With every splash, there's joy to share.
In this realm where laughter rings true,
Nothing is boring in the watery blue!

Beneath the Surface

Beneath the waves, a party's afloat,
With squids in tuxedos, they dance and gloat.
Clownfish giggle, wearing their stripes,
While anemones host with their floral gripes.

The sunken treasure is just a ruse,
It's a pirate's hoard of mismatched shoes.
Mermaids crack jokes, their laughter rings,
For the ocean holds all sorts of things.

Crabs wear hats, oh what a sight,
Joining the fun from morning till night.
Coral kingdoms host a grand ball,
Where guppies canoodle, and starfish enthrall.

Deep down below, the jesters play,
In a world where troubles just float away.
With bubbles of joy, we dive and play,
In laughter's embrace, we forever stay.

Celestial Reflections

The stars above wink at the sea,
While moonbeams giggle, wild and free.
Fish flash by in a twinkling race,
You'd think they're playing a game of chase.

A seagull swoops with a cheeky squawk,
Catching crumbs from our late-night talk.
The tide flows in like a sly old fox,
As crabs perform in their shiny socks.

Dolphins dive, with flips and spins,
Chasing the waves, they laugh, they grin.
A surfboard rides the glow of the night,
Under the moon's cheeky spotlight.

In the theater of waters, we find our bliss,
With every flip and splash, nothing's amiss.
So join the dance, let your spirit soar,
In this ocean's giggle, life's never a bore!

Beneath Rippling Shadows

Fishes swim in wobbly lines,
While crabs dance in fancy designs.
A starfish yells, 'I'm a sea star!',
But really, it's just a bit bizarre.

Seagulls swoop with chomping beaks,
Stealing fries and making squeaks.
The water laughs, a bubbling sound,
While mermaids trip; they fall, they bound.

Barnacles boast, stuck to their rocks,
'We're cooler than your flip-flop socks!'
They throw seaweed like confetti,
While dolphins bring snacks, all quite petty.

Bubbles float with giggling glee,
A jellyfish jives, moves so free.
"Ow, what's that sting?" a swimmer cries,
The sea just chuckles, "It's just a surprise!"

The Atlantic's Embrace

Waves come in, they foam and froth,
They tickle toes and tease the cloth.
A whale pops up with a cheeky grin,
Saying, "You really should try to swim!"

Seashells whisper tales so small,
Of pirates who once had a ball.
But truth be told, they lost the map,
And ended up in a big sea trap.

Octopuses play a game of hide,
While clams cheer on from the side.
"Let's make a splash!" a fish proclaims,
And boom, they're all part of the games.

Ocean breezes bring giggles galore,
As sandcastles sway and start to roar.
With every wave, there's laughter anew,
The sea's great fun, if you just knew!

Tranquil Horizons

Under the sun, a beach ball flies,
While seagulls mimic all kinds of cries.
A crab with shades moves in slow motion,
Pretending to surf on a small green ocean.

The hammock sways, a clever cat,
Tries to catch fish, but comes up flat.
With each tiny wave, a tickle and tease,
With popsicles melting, they aim to please.

Children giggle, the tide pulls away,
Grains of sand become part of their play.
A not-so-happy clam joins the show,
"Why can't I learn how to swim? Oh no!"

As sun sets down in a golden blaze,
Fish wear top hats amidst the waves.
"Let's dance tonight!" the ocean calls,
With laughter echoing through stone walls.

Enigma of the Surf

A tidal wave of giggles says,
"Can anyone tell me how to surf the rays?"
The seafoam laughs, in bubbling tones,
"Just jump on a wave, don't break your bones!"

An artist crab draws lines in the sand,
With a paintbrush made from a giant hand.
But the wind comes, swoops, and swirls,
"Oops, that's gone!" as the laughter twirls.

A turtle winks and moves so slow,
Dreaming of a race, but where to go?
"I'll hold the prize; it's all in jest!"
And off it plods, feeling quite blessed.

So join the fun, don't take it too hard,
Down by the surf, where giggles guard.
There's magic in each playful spout,
And laughter's what it's all about!

Echoing in Aqua Blues

The sea called me with a gurgling sound,
It begged for snacks and treasures abound.
I tossed in a pizza, but got back a fish,
With a wink and a flip, it made my day swish.

Seagulls cackled, like comedians on stage,
Diving for chips, turning a new page.
They squawked at my sunburn, a sight quite bizarre,
As I danced awkwardly, beneath a bright star.

The Silent Invitation

The tide rolled in with a giggly cheer,
It waved at my toes, saying, 'Come near!'
I thought it was greeting, oh what a faux pas,
For it pulled me in like a slippery spa!

Jellyfish floated, wearing hats made of foam,
They said, 'Join our party, you can call it home!'
I tried to boogie, but wobbled too wide,
The squishy sea pals just laughed while I tried.

Waves of Nostalgia

I found an old bottle, with a note snug inside,
Written by Mermaids, though they really just cried.
'We love your chips, please send us a meal!'
But they added, 'No pickles, that's really a deal!'

The shells giggled rumors, of crabs in a band,
Throwing a concert, so lively and grand.
I joined in the fun, but tripped on a rock,
While the seagulls all screeched, 'What a weird flock!'

Hidden Shores

In the shadow of seaweed, a treasure I found,
A pair of lost flip-flops, the best in the town!
I slipped them right on, but they sent me a dance,
With each silly shuffle, I took quite a chance.

Bubbles did tickle, as they popped with a cheer,
The starfish all clapped, said, 'He's quite the dear!'
With laughter they sang, a humorous score,
While I spun around, giving them encore.

Dreaming in Salt

Seagulls squawking, quite the show,
Waves are dancing, to and fro.
Crabs in shells, they peek and hide,
Jellyfish float like they glide.

Sunburned tourists, socks with sandals,
Ice cream cones, melting, quite the scandals.
Sandcastles crumble, a toddler's glee,
Who's laughing now? Oh, not just me!

Under the sun, we dare to play,
Surfboards wobble, 'Hey! Look my way!'
A crab steals lunch from an unsuspecting chap,
A seagull swoops in for the final clap!

With salty hair and sun-soaked skin,
We'll splash in puddles, let the fun begin.
Tides will rise, and sunsets glow,
We'll dance on shores where chuckles grow.

Whispers of the Seafoam

The waves are gossiping, take a seat,
Shells whisper secrets, oh so sweet.
Mollusks shuffle in a wavy stroll,
Playing tag with a curious shoal.

Fish in tuxedos, looking quite dapper,
Join the party, there's laughter and clapper.
Turtles in shades, lounging, enjoying the sun,
Sipping bubble tea, oh, what fun!

Sand dollars giggle, in their own way,
As if they know more about the day.
A dolphin jumps, aiming for grace,
But flops and splashes, a silly face!

Seashells chuckle, each crack a joke,
While little crabs prance, waking the folk.
With every wave, there's joy to behold,
A lilting laughter, stories untold.

Undercurrents of Solitude

Lonely starfish on a lonesome rock,
Counting the minutes, time to tick-tock.
But then comes a wave, oh, what a sight,
Bringing some joy in the pale moonlight.

A surf clam sighs, shells closed so tight,
Wishing for more than just quiet night.
But here come the bubbles, giggling away,
A frothy parade, come join the display!

A lone octopus issues a grin,
Yet flails its arms, oh, where to begin?
Whispers of currents, they tease and taunt,
While little fish giggle, just want to flaunt.

In solitude's depth, there's always a spark,
Laughter still echoes long after dark.
Even the seas have a jest to share,
In the silence there's joy, floating in air.

Lullabies of the Waters

Crashing waves, oh, what a tune,
Crooning to stars under the moon.
Splashing surf, a rhythmic beat,
A lullaby danced on sandy feet.

Moonlit jellyfish, serendipitous glide,
Whispering secrets as they slide.
Barnacles chuckle, clinging in place,
While silly dolphins put on their race.

Frolicking minnows in playful arrays,
Shimmering brightly, oh how they play!
With splashes and giggles, the water sings,
A symphony of joy that laughter brings.

Gulls on the shore, with antics so spry,
Dive in for snacks, oh my, oh my!
Each wave that crashes has stories to weave,
A lullaby of giggles, best believe!

Symphony of Waves

The waves dance high, they jump in glee,
Seagulls squawk their raucous spree.
Fish wear hats, they throw confetti,
While jellyfish play ring toss, all ready!

Crabs are drummers, tapping with flair,
Clams sing solos, without a care.
Starfish cheer, they wave all day,
As sea turtles join in, come what may!

A whale tries to swim but bumps the sand,
While dolphins form a conga band.
Splashing water, laughter profound,
Nature's party, all around!

Under the sun, not a worry in sight,
Every wave brings a new delight.
So let's dance and let worries cease,
In this symphony, we find our peace!

Secrets of the Abyss

Deep down below, where shadows creep,
The fish tell jokes, but they go 'neep!'
Octopuses spin tales of their fame,
While squids delight in the underwater game.

A clam plays chess, but loses the plot,
While eels give hairdos, like it or not.
The treasure chest has a mind of its own,
Jumping around, it won't be overthrown!

"Don't take my gold!" the pirate crab shouts,
But who'd want his loot? Just crumbs and doubts!
Bubbles float, carrying giggles and sighs,
The secrets below are all just disguise.

With laughter and fun, we dip and dive,
In the chilly blue where the quirks come alive.
So don your snorkel, come join the quest,
In the depths of the sea, adventures are best!

Beneath the Endless Sky

Beneath the sky, the waves leap high,
As fish wear sneakers and swim up to fly.
Crabs play poker upon the sand,
While seaweed shares a rock band!

Seashells gossip about the tides,
While playful otters wear life jackets with pride.
A pelican dives, but misses its snack,
And smacks in the waves, with a silly whack!

Whimsical whales hum a catchy tune,
While dolphins juggle beneath the moon.
With each splash and giggle, we find delight,
In nature's chaos, everything feels right.

So let's enjoy this seaside cheer,
Where laughter and joy are always near.
Bring your brightest hat, and don't look shy,
We'll dance with the fish beneath the sky!

The Call of Distant Shores

On distant shores where laughter bubbles,
Where sea creatures plot and cause trouble.
The wind whispers jokes that tickle your ear,
As sandcastles giggle, "We're top of the pier!"

Waves try to break but just want to hug,
While starfish wear scarves, cozy and snug.
A sand crab juggles shells in the sun,
And all through the day, it's just so much fun!

Seagulls are poets, their rhymes take flight,
While dolphins leap under the sparkly light.
The horizon's calling, with mischief in store,
As laughter rolls in from the faraway shore.

So grab your flip-flops and join the parade,
Where silly sea tales and fun are displayed.
With every soft splash, we can find our joy,
At the call of the waves, it's never a ploy!

The Serenity of Fathoms

In depths where fish wear party hats,
The seaweed dances, oh, imagine that!
A hermit crab with shades so bright,
Climbs a coral mountain, what a sight!

Jellyfish float like balloons in space,
Inviting all to join their race.
Starfish rave on the ocean floor,
Counting toes of divers, maybe four?

Turtles groove with a slow-motion twist,
While seagulls shout, "You can't resist!"
Bubbles rise like giggles in air,
Reef parties have no room for despair!

In this splashy bash, no one can frown,
As waves tease the shore, and laughter's the crown!

Hidden Songs of the Maritime

Sailors' whispers ride the sea breeze,
Got tales of fish that make them sneeze!
A clam hums tunes, slightly off-key,
While dolphins laugh in harmony!

Octopuses juggle with style and grace,
Throwing sea cucumbers all over the place!
A crab DJ spins—oh, what a mix,
Spawning joy with his silly tricks!

Corals flaunt colors like a painter's dream,
Pufferfish prank with a comical theme.
Mermaids giggle, flip hair with flair,
Salty jokes shared, add laughter to air!

Beneath the waves, where mischief runs wild,
The ocean hums, like a cheeky child!

Embracing the Ebb

Tides tumble in like a playful pup,
Scooping up seashells in a gleeful cup.
Mussels, clams, and barnacles jam,
Making music—oh, they are a band!

Waves hop like frogs on a sunny day,
Splashing your feet, come out and play!
Sandcastles crumble with a comical crash,
Seagulls swoop for a crumb, a quick dash!

The sun winks down, as if to say,
"Float on a noodle, it's a beach ballet!"
Kids laugh and giggle, chase after a seagull,
While a crab doffs a cap, looking quite regal!

Ebb-tide embraces, a funny old dance,
Where sea and shore give mischief a chance!

Calmness in the Storm's Eye

In the eye of the storm, fish play cards,
While waves are busy tossing the yards.
A whale drools while telling a tale,
Of mermaids with scales who flirt with a snail!

Flotsam bobbing like a cork in the chaos,
Seagulls squawking like they're the boss.
Puddles of rain become splendid slides,
Where sea turtles glide with the biggest grins wide!

Shark is a bouncer with a fierce-looking grin,
Saying "No entry!" to eels trying to get in.
The storm may roar like a lion, it's true,
But laughter's the balm to weather it through!

As clouds puff and blow, there's fun to be found,
Underneath the ruckus, joy knows no bounds!

Currents of Solitude

Once I swam with a fish so bright,
He told me jokes that gave me fright.
But all the laughter made me sink,
Now I'm just here, with time to think.

A crab passed by, in a sassy way,
He claimed he'd dance at the break of day.
But when the tide rose, he lost his groove,
Now we just chuckle as we try to move.

A dolphin leapt with a flip and a twist,
Said, "I'm a star in the sea, can't resist!"
But when I asked for a selfie quick,
He splashed me hard and made me sick.

In solitude's currents, humor flows free,
A wave of laughter, just fish and me.
We surf on joy, through thick and thin,
In this watery realm, we wear a grin.

Secrets in the Tides

Shell secrets chatter beneath the sea,
"You won't believe what's happening to me!"
A starfish claimed that he's quite a star,
But all he does is sit and spar.

An octopus dressed in purple attire,
Said, "Look at my tricks, I'm a performer!"
But all he did was squirt some ink,
And left us all with time to think.

Dancing waves keep secrets close,
As jellyfish glide, all snooty and gross.
They jive along with a sticky plume,
Wondering when they'll find a room.

In tides that tease and nudge our sides,
Lies laughter hidden where mischief hides.
From crabs to fish, we share our tales,
In a world where humor never pales.

Whispers of the Deep

The deep speaks softly with giggles and glee,
A seahorse struts, quite proud of his spree.
He wears a crown made of seaweed green,
Declaring himself the ocean's queen!

A whale's whispers are loud and meek,
"Why don't dolphins ever play hide and seek?"
"Because they'll just giggle and give you a clue,
And maybe even squirt you with their blue!"

Bubbles rise, with secrets they keep,
As turtles tell tales that make you weep.
"Did I ever tell you how slow I go?
I'm like a grandpa—out for a show!"

In depths where echoes bounce and dance,
Lies a world of laughter, mischief, and chance.
For in this watery place, we find some cheer,
Where whispers of the deep bring joy ever near.

The Calm Before Dusk

In twilight's calm, the sea takes a breath,
As sea otters delight in a game of chess.
They float on their backs with shells and a snack,
Plotting their heists, never looking back.

Gulls ponder long, debating the meal,
"Fish or chips?" they squawk with zeal.
But in the end, they just steal a fry,
And leave the fish wondering why.

The sun dips low, while seals have a ball,
Catching the rays and then taking a fall.
They giggle and splash in a sunset haze,
And ponder about their next goofy phase.

So before dusk claims the day's final laugh,
The sea holds its breath in a chuckling chaff.
With waves that tickle and whispers so sweet,
We revel in joy, in this twilight retreat.

Whispers on the Wind

Why did the crab cross the sandy lane?
To prove to the gull he could play the game!
With tiny pinches and wobbly claws,
He laughed at the waves, and chuckled with applause.

What do the seashells gossip about?
They trade fishy tales, no doubt!
With glistening hopes in the salty spray,
They plan a party for the jellyfish ballet.

A starfish wished on a moonlit beam,
Said, "I want legs, not just a dream!"
But once it was granted, it tripped all around,
Now it's the laughingstock, lost and confound.

The dolphins dance with splashes of cheer,
Inviting the turtles to join them here.
But the lazy old turtles just snored on the sand,
While the dolphins twirled, proud and unplanned.

The Language of the Waves

Can you hear the sea's winky winks?
It giggles and burbles; oh, how it jinks!
With bubbles of laughter and whispers so sweet,
It plays tag with the surf, oh what a feat!

The fish debate in a watery tongue,
About who is oldest, who's been most fun.
While the octopus paints with colorful flair,
Saying, "Look at my art! Come join if you dare!"

Seagulls squawk with a sassy twist,
Sharing the latest they simply can't miss.
Arranging a heist for some leftover fries,
While humans prize shells to adorn their eyes.

The tide rolls in, then rolls away,
Pulled by the moon in a cosmic ballet.
As laughter frolics across the blue,
The waves giggle softly; they're merry, it's true.

Twilight Over Tranquility

At sunset the starfish put on a show,
They wink at the sun, with an impressive glow.
The crabs in their tuxes, they tap dance with zest,
While sea cucumbers join, feeling quite blessed.

A clam opens wide, sharing secrets so bright,
Saying, "Do you see that? It's a seashell night!"
It invites all the fish for a glittery feast,
Rich with seagrass, the snacks never ceased.

The otters float by, exchanging a grin,
They'll juggle some shells, they're ready to win!
But one little flounder, shy in its stance,
Slips on a shell and starts a wild dance.

As twilight descends, giggles fill the air,
Creatures convene for festivities rare.
All around the shore, under stars shining bright,
They rendezvous laughing; oh, what a night!

The Secret Life Beneath

Beneath the waves, what mischief awaits?
The fishes throw parties, while crabs guard the gates.
With seaweed confetti, they dance without airs,
Swirling and twirling, without any cares.

Anemones giggle, tickling passing fins,
While clownfish crack jokes about life and sins.
The oysters all blush, all shy and demure,
As mermaids swim by, with tales to allure.

"Hey, have you seen my favorite shell?"
"It's pink, it's sparkly, oh, do tell!"
A search party forms, united in quest,
As laughter erupts, they're truly blessed.

With midnight drumming from a grouchy old bone,
The underwater critters make quite the scene.
Who knew beneath waves, life's fun could be found,
In bubbles and giggles, we frolic around!

A Tidal Embrace

The sea is a prankster, oh so sly,
Tickling toes as it rushes by.
It steals your hat with a giggling roar,
And leaves you laughing right on the shore.

Seagulls squawk with comedic flair,
Diving for snacks, without a care.
They plot and plan in the salty breeze,
For a chip or two, they'll do as they please.

The waves tease surfers with playful swoops,
Launching them high like slippery troops.
But gravity's cruel, they'll tumble and flop,
Waves roll in saying, "You'll never stop!"

Shells whisper jokes in the sparkling foam,
As beach balls dance, far from home.
The tide rolls out with a chuckle bright,
Leaving behind laughter, pure delight.

Beneath the Salt and Spray

Beneath the blue where the fish like to chat,
A crab tells jokes while wearing a hat.
"Stop shelling out wisecracks!" he cries with glee,
As the octopus giggles, just waving a sea.

The dolphins play poker, stakes are quite low,
A fishy surprise bursts from the flow.
They flip and they flop, making quite the scene,
With pearls as their chips, they're feeling quite keen.

Seaweed sways like it's grooving along,
While mermaids drown out their favorite song.
With each bubble popping, a laugh is let go,
As light sparkles in tides, putting on quite a show.

With a wink from a starfish, the day's still not done,
They joke about sea cucumbers having no fun.
Yet between all the laughter, one truth remains neat,
In the depths of blue, joy's the ultimate treat.

Mysteries of the Deep Blue

In the depths where the shadows play hide and seek,
A fish with a mustache begins to speak.
"Why did the octopus blush on that day?
Because it saw something too fishy to say!"

A whale tells tales loud enough to shake,
Of treasure chests filled with chocolate cake.
With a flap of its tail, it stirs the deep,
While jellyfish giggle, avoiding their sleep.

Mysterious bubbles keep popping with cheer,
As pirates complain, "Why's the rum always near?"
They search for the gold while the crabs laugh aloud,
"For real treasure's the friends that we're proud!"

As fish flash their fins in a harmless ballet,
They twirl and collide in a vibrant display.
With every swirl beneath the deep hue,
Life reminds us to laugh in the things that we do.

Gentle Caress of Waves

The waves come in like a cuddly hug,
Scooping up seashells, giving a tug.
"Hey, watch it now, I just found this one!"
With a swirl and a laugh, the day's full of fun.

Children build castles, getting quite bold,
Only to find the tide's a little too bold.
"Why did the moat dry up, you see?
Because it heard the waves shout, 'Come play with me!'"

Flip-flops fly off in a comical flight,
As seagulls swoop down, claiming the right.
A splash of cool water, a game of chase,
Laughter erupts, as they run with disgrace.

The sunset chuckles, wrapping up the day,
As the sky wears colors in a vivid display.
With a wink and a whistle, the waves bid adieu,
Silent laughter remains, just waiting for you.

The Luring Depths

A crab in a top hat danced on the sand,
He twisted and twirled, all part of his plan.
Seagulls were laughing, they'd never believe,
That crabs could throw parties, oh, let's not deceive!

The fish wore their sunglasses, so cool in the tide,
While dolphins did flips, taking style in their stride.
A clam played the accordion, what a big hit!
With barnacles clapping, they just couldn't quit!

Jellyfish tripped lightly, with floats in their hands,
They bounced on the waves, doing funky dance stands.
The starfish, quite dizzy, was stuck on a roll,
Saying, "Dance like a sea sponge, then save your sole!"

As waves giggled softly, they passed by the beach,
They whispered to creatures what nobody'd teach.
"Be silly and playful, it's the way of the brine,
Come join our strange party, it's way past divine!"

Silhouettes Against the Horizon

Seagulls were prancing, a comical sight,
Dressed in their feathers, all fluffy and bright.
While crabs started limbo, they swayed with the breeze,
The hermit crabs shouted, "I'll win with my knees!"

The sun took a dip, just for a quick tan,
As fish started gossiping, "Who's got the best flan?"
Octopuses juggled with shells and seaweed,
And laughed 'til they bubbled, what a grand deed!

A turtle, too slow, said, "Wait for my cue!"
But everyone charmed him with a conch hull boo-hoo.
While waves crash with laughter, the moon joined the jest,

And toast to those creatures who do what they best!

Horizons were dancing, their silhouettes grand,
Pretending to wrestle with the squishy land.
Their laughter resounded, as dusk turned to night,
With echoes of silliness taking brave flight!

Beneath the Surface

A fish with bubble glasses swam by with a flick,
He said, "Watch me, friends! I'm doing a trick!"
The octopus giggled, his ink made a mess,
"Next time, let's practice, I'll wear my best dress!"

Shells gathered together, sharing tales from afar,
Of seaweed that danced under a pale, glowing star.
"Did you see the crab?" they whispered with glee,
"Declaring his kingdom with absolute glee!"

Eels tangled up laughing, they too joined the game,
They swayed with the current, who's winning, not lame!
As sea cucumbers cheered from their cozy old nook,
They held little parties, each time they'd just cook!

Beneath the blue surface, there's fun to be found,
With friends all around, how could laughter not sound?
So come join the fun, where antics unfold,
In a world under waves, where stories are gold!

Echoes of Waves

The waves whispered secrets that tickled the shell,
They giggled and bubbled, like a wild carousel.
The sea horse themed parties caught all of the hype,
While angelfish snickered, "Let's start up the type!"

Crabs played charades, with a twist of a claw,
They mimicked the surfers, much to everyone's awe.
A narwhal held court, with a crown made of kelp,
"All hail our great ruler, the one with the help!"

Sandy shores echoed with laughter so bright,
As sandcastles strutted under moon's gentle light.
When fish threw confetti made from tiny shells,
They sang about bubbles with giggles and bells!

With memories echoing like waves on the shore,
Their fun unrelenting, they still asked for more.
So here's to the depths, where silly reigns supreme,
In the heart of the waves, where we dance and we dream!

Nightfall on the Sea

The fish wear pajamas, it's time for bed,
The seagulls are gossiping over their bread.
Starfish are dancing under the moon,
Crabs join the conga, oh, what a tune!

Jellyfish giggle as they float right by,
A dolphin tells jokes, oh me, oh my!
Waves roll in laughing, they tickle the shore,
While shells hold their breath, wanting more and more!

The night brings a party, no one's alone,
Even the octopuses have found a phone.
They scroll through selfies, saying "Look at me!",
As starry reflections dance in the sea!

With a splash and a splash, the fun has begun,
Nautical sketches, all drawn in the sun.
What a sight to see, in this oceanic play,
A raucous assembly, come join, don't delay!

Harmony of the Horizon

The sky stretches wide, like a canvas of blue,
Where dolphins are painters, it's true, it's true!
They swish with their tails, creating a scene,
With colors so vibrant, they make quite a scream!

Pelicans sing with a flair and a twist,
While octopuses juggle, no act can be missed.
The seaweed is swaying, like dancing on air,
As krill hum along without a single care.

Flip-flops are flopping across the wet sand,
A crab scuttles by, with a drink in his hand.
The sunset applauds, it's gold, red, and pink,
As creatures all gather, they sip and they wink!

In this comical realm, where laughter is loud,
Every wave whispers jokes to the crowd.
So come gauge the joy, on this cresting wave,
Where fun's always present and dolphins are brave!

Tides of Tranquility

The tide rolls in, with a bubbly surprise,
Seagulls play tag, soaring high in the skies.
A sea cucumber winks with a gleam in its eye,
As clam shells snicker, "Oh, my, oh my!"

Mussels tell stories of treasures they've seen,
While sand dollars blush at the sight of a bean.
Starfish spin yarns, oh, what a delight,
As crabs crack jokes in the soft moonlight.

With a splash, they invite you to join in the fun,
To collect all the shells, before day is done.
The laughter and joy, it dances on through,
As tides of delight give a wink just for you!

So take off your shoes, let your worries just float,
Join the merry band, on this whimsical boat.
In a world full of chuckles, the salt fills the air,
As tides of tranquility show how much they care!

A Whispering Depth

Bubbles of laughter rise up from below,
As mermaids are gossiping, putting on a show.
They braid up their hair with the kelp on the way,
And fish are their audience, what a parade!

Octopi in bow ties, looking quite neat,
Say stories of sailors who danced on their feet.
A shrimp shimmies by, laughing with glee,
As turtles slow dance, sipping fresh sea tea.

With coral so bright, they gather and cheer,
Each splash of the wave brings a delightful sneer.
Seashells give insights, wise under the wave,
While plankton float by, all feeling so brave!

So listen real close, as the depths share a jest,
In the rippling water, you know you're a guest.
With giggles and splashes, make memories keep,
In this whimsical realm, so vibrant and deep!

The Hushed Horizon

A wave wore a hat, quite absurd,
It tipped as it danced, oh how it stirred!
The seagulls all cawed with laughter so bright,
As fish in tuxedos swam out for the night.

A crab did a jig on the sun-soaked shore,
While sandcastles giggled, shouting for more.
With shells for their shoes and the tide as their band,
They formed a parade, the silliest strand.

A dolphin took selfies, a wave for a grin,
With treasures from divers all piled in a bin.
The octopus played hide and seek in his lair,
While jellyfish floated without a single care.

So come for a visit, the seaside's a blast,
Where the fun never ends, and the moments go fast.
With nature's own jesters all taking a bow,
The party's just starting, come join us right now!

A Serenade of Seashells

Seashells were singing a tune quite off-key,
With notes from the crabs dancing merrily.
The clam gave a wink, the conch blew a song,
As waves joined the choir, harmonies strong.

A starfish conductor waved all their limbs,
While barnacles clapped, enthralled by their whims.
"More glitter!" called out a bright little crab,
As lobsters performed in a glorious lab.

They played with the tides, a comedic charade,
With sea cucumbers that happily swayed.
"Encore!" shouted shrimps, and the audience cheered,
As mussels took turns, hoping they'd not be speared.

So listen, dear friend, to the songs from the sea,
For laughter and joy share a stage endlessly.
With laughter and music, the shores come alive,
In the festival's spirit, our hearts truly thrive!

Ripples in Time

A ripple once whispered, "I'm at your feet!"
A fish giggled back with a wiggly greet.
"Don't tickle my fins!" is what he exclaimed,
As bubbles took turns, all of them named.

A seahorse made bets with a turtle so slow,
While shrimp tried to dance, but fell in a row.
The dolphins were laughing, they jumped at the sun,
"Let's make a splash party, this is going to be fun!"

Jellyfish juggled and glided with grace,
As plankton cheered on from their comfy dark space.
The seaweed swayed gently, taking the floor,
In a whirlpool of antics, they begged for encore.

So when waves roll in with a tickle and tease,
Remember the joy of this dance with the breeze.
In life's crazy ocean, let humor be found,
For ripples of laughter are joyfully bound!

Surrender to the Depths

The depths hold wonders, a comical sight,
With creatures in costumes, a true delight.
The anglerfish winks with a glow for a laugh,
While eels in tuxedos swim past in a gaff.

A shipwrecked pirate, still searching for gold,
Found only a crab, who was cheeky and bold.
"Your treasure's my lunch!" said the crusty old mate,
While the parrot above laughed at their fate.

Anemones danced in the tickling tide,
As fortune-fish whispered, "You're always welcomed wide!"
With laughter and bubbles flowing through their domain,
They spun through the currents without any strain.

So dive in the splendor, where humor runs deep,
Where fish tell tall tales and laughter's a leap.
In the world's blue embrace, let giggles unfold,
For merriment thrives in the depths, brave and bold!

Where Shadows Dance

In the depths where fish take naps,
Octopuses pull funny pranks.
Seahorses wear tiny hats,
Mermaids roll their eyes at flanks.

Jellyfish float like balloons,
While crabs scuttle on the sand.
Seagulls squawk silly tunes,
Sandy toes create a band.

Starfish twirl with glee at night,
Dance moves that would make you cringe.
They shimmer with pure delight,
As waves roll in, they spin and cringe.

The tide brings laughter, echoes loud,
As barnacles tell their tales.
Growing old, still feeling proud,
In seaweed capes, all aboard the gales.

Songs of the Silent Deep

Bubbles rise like fizzy drinks,
Fish gossip under the waves.
They nibble on seaweed links,
And share secrets like little knaves.

Crabs wear glasses, oh so chic,
While eels perform the latest dance.
Turtle shells that squeak and creak,
All join in, given half a chance.

The dolphin choir sings off-key,
Hit those notes with quite a flair.
As whale choirs sing with glee,
The ocean chuckles in its air.

Sea creatures laugh as tides recede,
In bubbles, where voices steep.
They're having fun, that's guaranteed,
In this world, where secrets seep.

A Lullaby for Crashing Waves

Waves crash down with silly sounds,
They tickle shores with frothy foam.
The shoreline giggles, plays around,
As shells come clattering like a comb.

Surfers try to ride the tide,
Splashing water here and there.
Sealions bark with goofy pride,
While sea urchins dance with flare.

The tides take naps, then sing out loud,
Swaying gently, left and right.
Waves make a splash, a playful crowd,
Under the stars shining bright.

So take a seat and hear the call,
Of laughter mingling with the breeze.
The ocean tells a joke to all,
In riptides' rhythm, life's a tease.

Murmurs Beneath the Moon

The moon laughs at the ocean's play,
Casting glimmers on the waves.
Whales swim by, they seem to sway,
In moonlit gowns, they're like brave knaves.

Starfish whisper silly schemes,
To scatter sand like it's confetti.
Swaying creatures join the dreams,
In tides of jokes, both light and petty.

Crabby jokes circle the sea,
While fish wear tiny clown hats.
Seashells giggle, some agree,
Life here is full of laughs and spats.

As the stars wink and shine up high,
The sea breathes laughter soft and light.
With every tide, a joyful sigh,
Echoes beneath the moonlit night.

Embrace of the Abyss

Bubbles pop and fish do dance,
Jellyfish glide, giving it a chance.
Crabs do shuffle, wearing their best,
While seaweed sways, it's quite a fest.

Seashells gossip, but I can't hear,
They whisper secrets, full of cheer.
Starfish laugh as they lose their way,
In this wild aquarium, come what may.

Octopuses play games of hide and seek,
With a wink and a curl, they're quite unique.
Shoals of fish throw confetti with glee,
Who knew the deep could be so free?

Whales giggle in their submarine,
With a splashy show, they're quite the scene.
Under waves, it's a party galore,
Making memories, who could ask for more?

Shadows Under the Sea

In the deep, where shadows play,
Sea cucumbers dance in a quirky way.
Eels tell jokes with a wiggly flow,
While sardines shimmer like a disco show.

Crabs in tuxedos with scissors in hand,
Throwing a party, you'd never have planned.
Pirates shout, 'Not my treasure, please!'
As seagulls steal their sandwiches with ease.

Turtles slow-dance, but they're winning the race,
And dolphins surf with a smiling face.
Swirling underwater, what a delight,
Finding laughter from day to night.

Mysterious bubbles from deep below,
Pop with a giggle, and off they go.
A clever old otter claps his paws,
Declaring a toast to fishy laws!

Cradle of the Deep

Barnacles sing with a scratchy tune,
While seahorses prance under the moon.
Anemones wave like long-lost friends,
In this watery cradle, the fun never ends.

Clownfish burst out in a comic act,
With their goofy antics, they've got the knack.
Dolphins play catch with a seaweed ball,
While hermit crabs laugh as they trip and fall.

Coral reefs shimmer in all sorts of hues,
Playing hide-and-seek, oh what a ruse!
With a wink and a flip, they steal the show,
In this bustling cradle, come watch them glow.

Echoes of laughter in currents do weave,
Ever so clever, they never deceive.
Under the surface, joy is so steep,
Welcome aboard to the cradle of deep!

Songs of the Silent Shore

Seagulls squawk like they're at a rave,
While turtles groove with moves so brave.
The sand shells burst into joyous cheer,
As waves tumble in, tickling the ear.

Crabs do the cha-cha on sandy stages,
Flipping and flopping through all the ages.
A conch shell hums, it's quite the feat,
Its symphony made for dancing feet.

Pufferfish puff up, but they're full of jest,
Pretending to scare, but they can't contest.
A starfish winks at a ladybird,
As they share jokes, it's bliss unheard.

On the shore where secrets swish and swirl,
And undersea antics make laughter unfurl,
The music of nature, it surely implores,
To join in the dance on these sandy shores!

www.ingramcontent.com/pod-product-compliance
Lightning Source LLC
Chambersburg PA
CBHW060128230426
43661CB00003B/364